INDIAN FESTIVALS

INDIAN FESTIVALS

By Paul Showers

Illustrated by Lorence Bjorklund

Thomas Y. Crowell Company   New York

CROWELL HOLIDAY BOOKS

Edited by Susan Bartlett Weber

In the United States there are many different Indian tribes. There are Senecas and Seminoles and Sioux; Kiowas, Comanches, and Creeks. There are Navajos, Apaches, Cherokees, and Utes. They are all called Indians, but they are not at all alike. They are as different as their names.

Each tribe has its own ancient customs. Each tribe has the old language of its forefathers. And many tribes still keep special holidays and festivals when they recall the old ways of their ancestors with pride and thanksgiving.

One of the biggest holidays of the Seminole Indians in Florida is the Green Corn Celebration.

Late in June or in early July, the new corn stands tall and is ready to eat. Then the Seminole families pile into their cars and trucks and drive into the Everglades swampland. They drive past pools where alligators sun themselves and egrets and

herons guard their nests in the branches overhead. Far out in the swamp beside a broad meadow, the families set up camp under the trees.

Every night for nearly a week there is dancing around a big campfire. The men carry rattles made of cows' horns or tin cans filled with dried seeds. The women wear rattles under their long skirts. As the dancers move, the rattles mark the time:

shick   a-shick   a-shick   a-shick

Every afternoon the boys and girls play Seminole ball around a tall pole. The game is played with a deerskin ball stuffed with deer hair. Each team tries to hit the pole with the ball.

The boys cannot use their hands. They have to catch and throw the ball with rackets made of slender branches. When a team makes a hit, the score is marked on the pole.

On Picnic Day of the Celebration, the fires under the cooking pots blaze from sunrise until late at night. The feasting never stops. The favorite dish is a stew of beef, rice, and tomatoes.

The next day is Fast Day. The men and boys eat no food.

Early in the morning, the tribe's priest, who is called the Medicine Man, brings the magic Medicine Bundle from its secret hiding place in the swamp. The Bundle is the tribe's most precious possession. It is very old.

The Seminoles say it came to their fore-fathers from the Great Power that fills the universe. They believe the Bundle has power in itself to keep the tribe strong and healthy. They say the tribe will die if the Bundle is ever harmed or lost.

The Medicine Bundle is wrapped in deerskin. Inside are many smaller deerskin bundles. They hold sacred things—magic stones and magic powder, dried roots and herbs, bits of horn and bone, feathers, snake fangs.

Few people have ever seen these things. Only the Medicine Man dares to touch them. He opens the Bundle and makes sure that none of the sacred objects are missing. He says a long prayer. Then he ties up the Bundle again and hangs it on a forked stake at the edge of the dance ground.

All during Fast Day the Bundle hangs

on the stake. At noon the men gather in the open-air arbor they have built near the campfire. There they hold a council to discuss the tribe's affairs and to settle disputes. Later that day there are dances.

At sunset the Medicine Man takes the Bundle and lays it reverently on the ground near the great campfire. All that night, while the flames leap high into the sky, the men and women of the tribe dance before the sacred Bundle.

Many Seminole dances imitate the movements of birds or animals. There is the Buffalo Dance, the Chicken Dance, the Alligator, the Catfish. At midnight of Fast Day the Seminoles perform the Green Corn Dance.

This is the sacred dance of their forefathers. The men chant the old words as they dance. The words are so old that

now nobody remembers what they mean.

But everybody knows what the Green Corn Dance means. It is an ancient prayer to the Great Power of the universe to protect the Seminoles, to keep the tribe and the Medicine Bundle strong during the coming year.

The old chant makes the dancers feel good. They remember that the tribe has had many hardships but it has never been destroyed. They remember they are Seminoles, and they feel strong and ready to face the world again.

At dawn the women hurry back to the family campfires to prepare the last great feast. The Medicine Man opens the Medicine Bundle and counts the sacred objects once more. He says another prayer. Then he ties it up and takes it back into the swamp.

The food is laid out in the arbor. For

the first time during the Celebration there is corn to eat—fresh boiled corn on the cob, corn gruel to drink, and big flat corn biscuits fried in a pan. Everybody is hungry.

The Medicine Man's helper watches the swamp. At last he sees the Medicine Man returning empty-handed. That means the sacred Bundle is safely hidden once more.

Now the meal can begin. Everybody starts eating. For the Seminoles, this is the beginning of a new year.

Almost all Indians raise corn. The Zuñi Indians of New Mexico grow it in the desert country where they live. Rain falls there only a few times during the year. Every drop is precious. Without rain the corn will not grow. There will be no grass for the tribe's sheep to feed on.

For hundreds of years the Zuñis have

said prayers to the rain spirits. They have also honored the Shalako, who are the messengers of the rain spirits.

One of the great Zuñi holidays is the Shalako festival, when chants and prayer dances are performed.

Certain men of the tribe are chosen to be the dancers. During the festival they will wear masks. They will pretend to be

the rain spirits and the Shalako and other spirits the Zuñis honor.

All year long the Zuñis prepare for the big celebration. From time to time the men who are to dance go to secret shrines in the desert. There they pray to all the spirits. They practice the sacred chants and dances.

As festival time nears, they paint the masks with fresh colors. There are six huge Shalako masks, with eyes and beaks that move. Each mask is carried on a tall pole by a dancer. His body is hidden by the mask's long skirt.

The Shalako dancer has tiny bells tied to his knees. When he runs, the bells jingle. He pulls hidden strings and the big eyes of the mask turn. He pulls another string and the great beak goes *snap-snap*.

The festival is held around the first of

December. The village, or pueblo, is crowded with visitors from other tribes and with tourists. The Zuñis wear their best clothes. Everybody waits for the spirits to enter the pueblo.

First comes a boy dancer with a burning branch. His body is painted black with colored spots. He wears a mask. This is Shulawitsi, the fire spirit.

With him comes a man who carries a basket full of sticks with feathers tied to them. These are the sacred prayer plumes that are used in the ceremonies.

Next come the rain spirits in buckskin and beads, with bright, striped masks. As they pass through the crowd, the Zuñis sprinkle them reverently with sacred corn meal. Then the spirit dancers go into the house of Sayatasha, the rain spirit of the north. There they say prayers in private.

At sunset the Shalako dancers come running across the desert to the pueblo. The great masks seem to fly over the ground. The eyes roll. The beaks snap. Behind the masks the dancers make sharp cries like birds.

In the pueblo, houses are ready to receive the six Shalako. Some of the houses are brand-new. Others have a fresh coat of plaster inside. The owners welcome the Shalako into the new houses. A visit by a Shalako is a great honor.

All that night the Zuñis pray with chants and dances, asking the spirits not to forget to bring them rain. The visitors crowd into the houses to watch and listen.

The men of the tribe chant prayers while the Shalako dance from one end of the room to the other. It is hard work.

The dancers dare not stumble or miss a step or they will bring bad luck.

At dawn the chanting stops. The dancers take a rest. Then at noon everyone in the tribe lines up to say farewell. As the dancers leave the pueblo, the Zuñis sprinkle sacred meal on them once more.

That night more masks are brought out. All night long and for three nights more there is dancing, until every man in the tribe has put on a mask and danced a prayer.

Indians sometimes borrow one another's ceremonies. On the Great Plains and in the Rocky Mountain country, the Sun Dance is performed every year by a number of tribes. The Utes and Shoshones, the Crees and Sioux and Cheyennes, all hold Sun Dances in the summer when the sun is high and the days are hot.

One man in the tribe has a dream. It tells him to hold a Sun Dance. This makes him the leader. He tells the other men, and they help him build the lodge for the dance.

A Sun Dance lodge is a kind of open-air house. A circle of poles is set up around a tall center pole. Roof poles connect the center pole and side poles. Brush is piled up to make the walls of the lodge, and a stuffed buffalo head is hung from the center pole.

Only a few men in the tribe actually join in the Sun Dance. It is a long, hard test of strength. A man dances because he believes it will bring him good luck or a long life. Sometimes he has a disease and hopes the dancing will cure it.

The dancers prepare themselves by bathing in a stream. Sometimes they paint their faces and bodies. Each man wears

an eagle-bone whistle around his neck. During the dance he blows on the whistle from time to time.

The dancers and their friends enter the lodge at sunset. The friends come to watch, to help sing the sacred chants, and to beat the big drum. The leader and the dancers say a prayer. A fire is lighted. The men sitting around the drum begin beating time. The singers start the chant. The dance begins.

The dancers jog forward to the center pole in time to the drum. Then they jog backward to the lodge wall, still facing the center pole. Forward and back they dance.

That night, and for the next two days and two nights, the dancing goes on. When

the drummers tire, others take their places. The singers take turns chanting the songs. But the weary dancers do not halt.

They take time to rest only in the morning. Each day at dawn the dancers stop to pray to the rising sun. Then they sleep for about an hour while their friends go out to eat breakfast.

The dancers eat nothing during a Sun Dance. Through the long, hot days they take only little sips of water. They grow hungry and very thirsty. In the last hours of the dance they often faint from weariness. But they get up and struggle on.

On the morning of the third day, the drumming and chanting stop. The dancers go to the stream and bathe. After that they eat watermelon and drink bottle after bottle of soft drinks to end their terrible thirst.

The Sun Dance is over.

Some Indian tribes have harvest celebrations after they have gathered their crops. The Eskimos in Alaska have a special holiday after a successful whale hunt.

In the spring when the ice begins to break up in the sea, the men put out in small boats to hunt whales. It is dangerous work, for the boats can be wrecked on the ice floes in the half-frozen sea.

Whenever a boat crew makes a kill, the

dead whale is hauled up on the ice. Every man gets a share of the meat.

After the hunt is over, the boats are dragged from the water and turned on their sides to make a shelter from the icy wind. Then the captains and crews who have caught whales give a party.

There are good things to eat and tea to drink. All the neighbors are invited.

It is the custom for the men to bring

out a big piece of walrus hide and toss
each other on it. When they all heave
together, they can toss a man twenty feet
in the air. He does his best to keep his
balance and come down feet first. One
after another, the men test their skill at
this sport.

In the afternoon there is dancing. Five or six men sit around a big drum and beat time. A chorus of men and women chants the songs.

First the boat captains and their wives and crews dance. Then the other men and women of the village join in. The fun goes on until late at night.

Sometimes several Indian tribes hold a big celebration together. Every summer people from the Kiowa, Comanche, Delaware, Osage, Pawnee, Apache, and other plains tribes hold a fair.

They come in cars, trailers, and pickup trucks to the town of Anadarko in Oklahoma. Some come from homes hundreds of miles away. At the fairgrounds in Anadarko they pitch their tents and teepees or build arbors of brush as their forefathers did.

The fair lasts for a week. There is a merry-go-round and a Ferris wheel. There are games of chance and refreshment stands.

Every afternoon and evening, people of the different tribes take part in races and dance contests before the grandstand.

In the horse races, the young Indians ride their beautiful horses bareback.

The dancers are of all ages. They wear fine costumes of feathers and deerskin and perform the ancient dances of their ancestors.

These are not sacred dances. They are contests. Judges are chosen from each tribe. They watch the dancers and give prizes to the best ones.

Later in the summer thousands of Indians gather at another big fair at Gallup in New Mexico. Here, too, there are races

and dance contests. The Indians show the beautiful rugs and pottery and jewelry they have made by hand.

Indian fairs of this kind are a time for fun and play. They also attract tourists from all over the United States. The tourists come to watch the races and the contests and to buy souvenirs.

But the true Indian holidays are the old

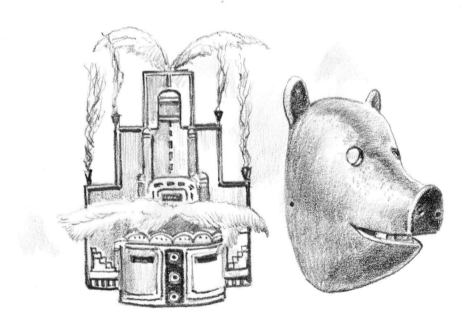

celebrations. Visitors are sometimes welcome, but most old Indian holidays are private.

They are a time for worship and for old sacred customs. The people of the tribe chant the songs of their forefathers. They perform the ancient dances.

As they sing and dance, they feel the spirits of their forefathers are still with them. It makes them feel strong and safe.

ABOUT THE AUTHOR

Paul Showers has been interested in American Indian culture ever since a family camping trip to Arizona and New Mexico. On that first visit he saw the Santo Domingo pueblo perform its magnificent Corn Dance. Before beginning *Indian Festivals,* Mr. Showers reread his collection of books about American Indians, corresponded with Indian agencies, and dug into anthropological papers at the Museum of the American Indian in New York City.

A member of the staff of *The New York Times,* Mr. Showers has been a newspaperman and writer since his first job with the Detroit *Free Press.* He was born in Sunnyside, Washington, received his B.A. degree from the University of Michigan, and now lives with his family in suburban New Jersey.

ABOUT THE ILLUSTRATOR

When Lorence Bjorklund was a child in St. Paul, Minnesota, he loved to sit on a bluff overlooking the Mississippi River. Here, close to burial mounds of Indian chiefs, he daydreamed about the pioneers and Indians who were to figure so prominently in his work as an artist.

Mr. Bjorklund has illustrated well over three hundred books, most of which are based on an Old West theme. His hobbies are closely associated with his work, for he collects guns, builds scale models of ships and wagons, and studies Indians at remote camps in the United States and Canada.

Mr. Bjorklund and his family live in Croton Falls, New York, and spend their summers in Maine.